I0521849

I Am Sheikh Mujib

An Epic Monologue

Anisur Rahman

Translated by
Anisur Rahman with Zaheer Ahmed

Dracopis Press

www.dracopis.com

beard@dracopis.com

Dracopis_009
Anisur Rahman: I Am Sheikh Mujib; An Epic Monologue

ISBN 978-91-87341-14-4
EUROPE: Printed by Ingram Spark, UK, 2021
USA: Printed by Ingram Spark, USA, 2021

Editions:
ISBN 978-91-87341-13-7 (Hardcover)
ISBN 978-91-87341-14-4 (Softcover)
ISBN 978-91-87341-15-1 (E-book)

© 2021 The Writer, the Translators, and Dracopis Press
Published by Dracopis Press, Sweden, 2021. All rights reserved

Translated from Bengali by Anisur Rahman with Zaheer Ahmed
Edited by Melanie Perry and Dominic Williams

Cover Illustration by Rafiqun Nabi
Insert ilustrations by Nisar Hossain

We would like to thank
Md Moshiul Azam Shajal, Dhaka.

Dedicated to the memory of Mahatma Gandhi (1869-1948)

A tale of dark days in prison for fighting for freedom and justice. This monologue brings back the voices of people whose heritage is located in the Indian Subcontinent. I am inspired to seek out those people once more, to share and discuss this captivating piece of writing. Anisur Rahman's energy, attention to time and place, personal connection and knowledge of the changes in 20th Century India give this apposite monologue gravitas and agency.

The piece traces the political and cultural basis for, and impact of, the creation of Pakistan and ultimately an independent Bangladesh. From the perspective of Sheikh Mujib, much of the monologue is set during his many prison terms as he reflects on his life from the late 1930s to the mid 1970s. He considers his move through activism and politics, and his role in the fight for a fair and just Bengal for Muslims and Hindus. The foundation of his sickly childhood, the aspirations he shares for his own children, and his concern to support the vulnerable are integral lights in his humanity.

> *I am a man for works.*
> *What I think, I try to do it.*
> *I made mistakes, I corrected them.*

Whether you read this on the page, or hear the voice in performance, I am sure that you will be moved by this personal insight into the major political struggle and change that helped create Bangladesh.

Melanie Perry

I Am Sheikh Mujib

Huseyn Shaheed Suhrawardy.
I remember him in this lonely prison.

How could he extend his hands of blessing towards me?
How could I get in touch with him?
On which morning?

He introduced me to many paths of politics in our country.
I also remember my eye operation in the operating theatre
at Calcutta Medical College.
Since the operation I have begun to use glasses.
I dropped out from study because of my illness.
Then I fell behind in my schooling for a few years.
I had nothing to do.
I had no work.
I did not study.

Everyday I was drawn towards the Swadeshis, native activists
for freedom.
I became fond of Subhash Bose's party.

At that age, I realised that the English have no right to run
this country.
I attended the meeting of the Swadeshis.
I travelled between Gopalganj and Madaripur.
The Madaripur sub-district's chief warned my grandfather.

My experiences as a boy should have prepared me for the consequences.

People who disrupt a good initiative, ultimately deserve trouble.

When we were students we used to collect rice as aid for poor students.
We looked for accommodation for poor students.
My interest in activism grew and grew.

How I could be a daring boy..?

But illness hampered my study for four years.

I thought, if an opponent party member beats any member of our party, we should punish the attackers.

How could I become the powerful leader of this daring group?

People complained against me to my father.

Bengal's Chief Minister A.K. Fazlul Huq and Labour Minister Suhrawardy made a visit to Gopalganj.
I was the leader of a volunteer group.
Hindu boys began to revolt and engage in non-cooperation.
What was the reason?

The Congress Party had asked them not to cooperate.

Why? What was the reason behind it?

Mr. Huq is a Muslim, Mr. Suhrawardy is a Muslim.
For the first time, I realized, I was disappointed.
I had not thought of this before, I could not figure it out.
I could not even imagine it.

Hindus and Muslims are the same people, we are equal.
What is the difference between us?

Mr. Suhrawardy noted down my name and address.
After his return, he sent me a letter to which I responded.

The Police arrested us and imprisoned us.

My first period in jail was in 1938.
That was the fate of the Bengalis.
If someone captured any of our party members, we would
bring him back with a strong fight.

In 1939,
I met Mr. Suhrawardy in Calcutta.
After my return to Gopalganj from Calcutta, I dedicated
myself to expanding our party.

Despite my illness, I passed my exams.

How could I study?

I spent my time in politics, in meetings.
My father did not have any objection to sports and politics,
but he wanted me to concentrate on my studies as well.
I was convinced that we must establish Pakistan, as a state
for Muslims.

Otherwise, the Muslims would not have freedom.
I was convinced by whatever the Azad newspaper wrote.

In 1941,
The Convention of the Chhatra League in Faridpur was
attended by poets Kazi Nazrul Islam, Humayun Kabir, and
principal Ibrahim Khan.
The government declared Section 144, we all realised that we
would not have any freedom unless we established Pakistan.

Despite their time as students ending,
student leaders continued to occupy posts in student
organizations —

What could be expected from such leaders?

In 1943,
Bengal was witnessing a dangerous famine.

Thousands of hungry people were migrating towards towns
from villages.

They had nothing to eat.
They had no clothes to wear.
The English had cancelled all trips by boats and had seized all
the storage for paddy and rice.
Businessmen were using the situation to chance their luck and
exploit people.

They sold one packet of rice for 50 taka, when the original
price was only 10 taka.
Ordinary people were abandoned on the streets.

They were half-fed.
They were un-fed.

Mr. Shaheed Suhrawardy was Supply Minister,
and thus he gained a poor reputation with people.
Mr. Shaheed Suhrawardy tried his best, and opened gruel
kitchens in villages.

He collected rice, wheat and flour.

The English thought "if people die of hunger, let them die."
Support for war was the first priority, goods required firstly
for war.
After that, if there was any empty space left on trains, it could
be used to carry food for people.

For shame! For shame! For shame!
The evil British who created such famine in Bengal.
Following the advice of Mr. Shaheed Suhrawardy,
leaving my study, I engaged myself to save famine-affected
people.
I helped take care of hungry people day and night.
My health collapsed.

I had married Renu in my boyhood,
but we had our ceremony for sleeping together on a bed of
flowers in 1942.

Thus then, Renu took care of me and I recovered.

How could I forget it?
If your pledge in life is true, you will not lose.

Many people secretly denigrated me to my father.
They wanted to turn my father against me.
My father was confident in my involvement in politics,
so I devoted myself to that.

My father discussed politics with me, asking me many
questions.
"Why do we want to establish the state Pakistan?
What will be the ultimate result of our movement?"
I responded to his questions elaborately.
"If we do not get Pakistan, how will the Muslims in Bengal
survive?"

As soon as I attempted to say something about Mr. Huq's
politics, I faced a troublesome situation.
My father forbade me.
My mother forbade me.
Village people suggested to me that whatever I wanted to
say was welcome, but never try to say anything negative
about A. K. Fazlul Huq.
We had to present our arguments for the Pakistan movement
in another way.

We wanted to establish Pakistan.
We wanted not only one Pakistan,
we wanted two Pakistans — one should be Pakistan in the West,
the other should be Bengal in the East.
Both the Hindus and the Muslims would live in our Pakistan.
I had learnt from the Sepoy Revolution.
I had learnt from Titumir, Shariatullah.
I had learnt from the movements of the Faqirs and the
Sannyasins.

My friend Nani Kumar Das lived at his paternal uncle's home.
He often visited our home.
I also used to visit him at his uncle's home.
One day Nani was weeping and telling me that his aunt had
been angry with him.
She got him to clean their house since as a Muslim boy I made
a visit to their home.
I am a Muslim boy.
I was disappointed.
Thus, I told Nani, I would not go to his home.
"You are welcome, you are welcome, my brother Nani," I
added.

Many Hindus were put in jail.
Many Hindus also were hanged.

In this way, both the Hindus and the Muslims had shared the
same pains and dreams.

In spite of this, the two communities could not be united.
Nobody had tried to unite them.
Some however came to realize indeed...
Chittaranjan Das and Subhas Bose had been considerate
about the Hindus.
But the Hindus in Bengal had not realized, had not accepted it.

This way, the Hindus and Muslims departed along two
different paths.
Mr. Hashim presented his logic to unite the Hindus and the
Muslims.
He tried his best to convince the people:
Pakistan did not mean to be against Hindu.

Pakistan meant that both the Hindus and the Muslims could live together in harmony.

There was a Muslim League Convention in Delhi.
Muslim leaders from the entire Indian Subcontinent were invited to Delhi.
I was madly curious to see the Red Fort, the Qutub Minar, the Jame-i Mosque in Delhi.

I decided that I would make a visit to Nizamuddin Auliya's mausoleum.

I set off from Calcutta towards Delhi with strong hope.
Mr. Jinnah and other leaders were due to deliver their speeches.

In this dark solitary jail
I remember Mr. Suhrawardy.

Once I showed my anger to Mr. Suhrawardy and he came out of his home.

I was so angry, I was so upset, I just wept.

Mr. Suhrawardy took me back.

He hugged me and expressed his affection for me.
He put his hands on my head, and I received affection from him.

He is a lion-hearted human being, with a great mind.
I know Mr. Suhrawardy with my heart.

Mr. Hashim's manifesto drew heavy attention and response from towns and the countryside.

The Zamindari system would be abolished.
It would be a great thing.
We did not pay any attention to our studies.
We engaged ourselves in party activities by day and at night.
What would we have done with our studies if we had failed to establish Pakistan?

Shame on Marwari businessmen!
For making a heavy profit, they hid food and textile at their storehouses.

They created artificial crises for food and clothes.

They began to make ten times the profit compared to real prices of food and clothes.

Mr. Suhrawardy noticed it.
He ordered a raid in the Lal Bazar area and recovered thousands of yards of textile.
People became angry and attacked the Marwari businessmen.

The Marwari businessmen were strong though.
They bribed the Legislative Assembly Members and had the Muslim League government ousted from office.

Could it be possible?

The Marwari businessmen wearing pagri and tupi
demonstrated and rejoiced on the streets in Calcutta.
One day along with my group of fellow party activists,
I attacked a group of Marwari businessmen.

What a beating it was...

I could not think of it... how the leaders could take bribes
this way?

And the fate of people and country in the hands of these
leaders...

We were students,
we loved our country.
We dedicated ourselves to the future of our country.

Yet, those Khan Bahadur leaders would establish Pakistan!
It was difficult for me to believe it:

They would free the country!
They would drive away the English!

I could not believe it.
It was difficult for me to believe.

I did not see any hope.
Mr. Khan, Bengal's landlord Khan Bahadur, having title from
the British, he had not founded Pakistan.
Bengal's peasants had not supported them.
The people in Bengal did not trust them.

Bengal's people, Bengal's farmers had supported
the Muslim League.
They had accepted the words of Mr. Suhrawardy and
Mr. Abul Hashim.

We felt a national rage towards the English.
If the English were defeated, it would be the ultimate revenge.

How I could I support the misdeeds of Hitler?

But, wherever the English were defeated, I somehow felt good
in my mind.
We had become tired of English oppression.
How could we forget it?
We were not for the English,
we were not for Hitler.
So I thought, "If we could have Subhas Bose here today, our
country could be freed."
How great it could have been.
I thought at the same time:
Could it be good for the Muslims?

I thought again… when a leader leaves everything at home to
stay abroad and fight for the freedom of his country…
he could never be communal as a leader.
Subhash Bose delivered his speech from Singapore.

I listened to his speech and became excited.
I waited for that good day.
Would it give us freedom, as the English would be expelled
and the Japanese would get in?
No!

No!

No! Never!

I was afraid at the thought of how Japan attacked China.

"I am still afraid of this."

We wanted our freedom.

We wanted to expel the English.

We wanted to have independent flags for India and Pakistan in the Indian Subcontinent.

Hindus and Muslims would live here together.

Muslims and Hindus would sing the same song in the Pakistani part.

Muslims and Hindus would sing the same song in the Indian part.

Pakistan does not mean harm to the Hindus.

India does not mean any harm to the Muslims.

I do not tell a lie.

I cannot cheat.

That is why I speak my mind.

I do not want to make any difference between the rich and the poor.

I am outspoken and tell the truth.

I am not nervous, honesty is my path.

I know there is no newspaper in this country that carries our story.

We all worked hard by day and night.

I am a workaholic.

I am not the type to avoid work and listen to scholarly discussions.

I did not want to be a scholar.
That is why I could not attend the scholarly classes for hours
and hours at night.
You could not get me into such a class.
I will never flee from work.
I will never flee from life.

I encountered both meanness and openness in politics in
my student life.
In the beginning I recognised Mr. Suhrawardy as a symbol
for greatness.
On the other hand, Mr. Khawja Nazimuddin was the opposite.

It is better to face the truth in life and politics rather than to flee from it.
To flee from the truth is mean, cowardly and evil.

Mr. Suhrawardy had to face such bad elements in politics.

To have self-confidence is very important.

Mr. Suhrawardy had proven it many times.
Though, he had had to accept defeat many times by ill-willing
people.

Bengali Muslims have two qualities: Muslim and Bengali.
We are fond of finding faults in others.
We cannot be happy at the goodness of others.
We cannot enjoy the good news of others.
We cannot accept the good news of others.
We can be convinced by good dress and eulogizing words.
If someone wears a cap or pagri, we accept him as a religious
leader, peer.

We salute him.
But that so-called peer may not know anything about religion.
But the Bengalis will not look into it.
That is why they are cheated.
The Bengalis remain poor; they remain dominated.
Despite having many resources and qualities the Bengalis are
exploited, the Bengalis remain poor.

The British are really British.
They carried the blood-line from Robert Clive, the pioneer
colonizer.
How could they be detached them from this 'Clive' heritage?
After the Second World War, their original aim was to help
chaos continue in the Indian Subcontinent.
They wanted to make the Congress Party happy.
They wanted to deny our movement for Pakistan.

Democracy means the majority party leader will run the country.
But the opinions from a minority party are also to be respected and
logical opinions are to be accepted.
The base of democracy and justice lies there.
Shame on the British — coal never changes its colour.

We were travelling to Delhi, our train stopping at every station.
Passengers waited to see Bengal's Prime Minister Mr.
Suhrawardy and listen to his speech.
They were waiting to hear him.
If the train had not stopped and Mr. Suhrawardy had not
spoken, the waiting people would have been disheartened.

Would it have been acceptable?

Sheikh Mujib, painting by Nisar Hossain.

I saw Delhi and thought that the British would leave.
The Indian Subcontinent would be independent.
We would have no duty to Delhi.

The Red Fort, the Qutub Minar and the Jame-i Mosque are
unique testimonies to the Muslim arts in Delhi.
Ajmer Sharif City was built around a large lake.
On one side are the signs of Mughal era.
Most of the testimonies are from Emperor Shah Jahan's era.
I wished that I could have lived in Ajmer Sharif.
It was forbidden for people to live there.
The idea was that "Who will free us if the police arrest us
here in this foreign city at night?"

We decided that Pakistan was our demand.
But this demand was not against the Hindus.
This demand was for access to the rights of the people
in Bengal — both the Hindus and the Muslims.
This demand was for independence.
This demand was for all religions.
This demand was for establishing rights of all people.

Let the British leave.
Let imperialism be vanquished.
Let our Indian Subcontinent be free.

One human being and one beast exist in each man.
Calcutta witnessed communal riot in 1947.
Whenever the Hindus found a Muslim, they attacked him.
The Muslims acted in the same way.
At the same time, a group of Muslims tried to save a group
of Hindus, or a group of Hindus save a group of Muslims.

Who fights against whom?
Who makes attacks on whom?
One brother beats the other.
Another brother saves the victim.

Following Calcutta, Noakhali witnessed riot,
subsequently, riot spread to many other places.

What could we do?
Where could we go?
I went to Boira and Asansol.
After helping the riot-affected people, I returned to Calcutta.
By that time I had become ill.

The politics in Indian Subcontinent were complex.
The British would survive if they could flee.
But how?

It was June 1947.
It was declared;
The Congress Party agreed;
The Indian Subcontinent was to be divided.
They wanted to gain by splitting Bengal.
Two parts of Bengal: India would get one part and Pakistan
would get the other.

On behalf of Mr. Suhrawardy, his Finance Minister Mohammad
Ali had declared that Calcutta would be the capital of Bengal.
Alas! He was neither aware, nor could we guess the fact.
They used the knife on the fate of Bengal.
Calcutta had been given to India.

Mr. Suhrawardy, Mr. Hashim and Mr. Sarat Bose went to
Delhi with a demand for a separate Bengal.
Mahatma Gandhi did not say a word,
neither did Nehru.
Patel cheated with them.
They dishonoured Sarat Babu.
He told Sarat Babu to leave his madness for Bengal.
The Governor Mountbatten was secretly working for the
Congress Party.
He dreamed of holding the position as governor for both
Pakistan and India at the same time.

It was impossible to fathom the cheating committed by
the British.
The calculation was easy.
The population in Bengal was bigger than in the entire
Pakistan.
Mr. Suhrawady would be the Prime Minister and Mr. Jinnah
appreciated him.
So conspiracy had begun against him.
Thus Mr. Jinnah died, due to this conspiracy, and Pakistan
became one and equal.

To err is human.
I make mistakes too.
I confess my mistakes and make the correction.
Nothing wrong in that.

Mr. Suhrawardy and Mr. Mahatma Gandhi travelled to
Barakpur.
I joined them.

Gandhi ji recited from the Quran, then he read from the
Ramayana.
Following the speech of Gandhi ji, the crowd made the slogan,
'Hindu-Muslims are brothers of each other.'
Really Gandhi ji knows magic.

The people who are active, they have a possibility to make mistakes.
The people who avoid working, they have no risk of making
mistakes.
They are of no use when it is needed.
I am a man for works.
What I think, I try to do it.
I made mistakes, I corrected them.

The Indian Subcontinent was divided into two parts.
Gandhi ji along with Mr. Suhrawardy hosted public meetings
in different places all over the Indian Subcontinent.

How long would Gandhi ji protect Mr. Suhrawardy?
The Hindus wanted to kill him.
They attacked him several times.
They threw bombs at his home.
Despite this, Mr. Suhrawardy would not come here and leave
Calcutta.

We had to work in East Bengal to check for any possible riot.
Mr. Suhrawardy was the only leader who dared to visit to
Punjab, Delhi, or Jeypore to witness the riots.

After the end of British rule in the Indian Subcontinent
Mr. Suhrawardy came to East Bengal.
He was to deliver a speech at a public meeting in Barisal.

No leader in the All Muslim Chhatra League had their
studentship.
The committee was formed in 1944.
Since we founded Pakistan, it was time to start a new
organization.

Everyone in the East Pakistan Muslim Chhatra League was
a king.
Oli Ahad objected to the word 'Muslim'.
I told him what was significant in a name.
We had just got Pakistan.
If we could uphold our ideology and policy, we would be able
to change the name later on, I pointed out.
Policy, ideology and work were the basic issues.

Politics in Pakistan began to turn in wrong directions at
every step.
Conspiracy against Bengal began.
First, they attacked our language and culture.
They were forcibly trying to make Urdu the state language,
denying Bengali as the majority people's language.

How were we inferior to them?
They must also accept Bengali as the state language of
Pakistan.
We protested at this initiative.
We had our Language movement.
Many of us were arrested.
Holy Pakistan began to be unholy at every step.
A group of false leaders and bureaucrats were gaining benefit
all the way.

There were many school students among the arrestees from the Language movement.
One of them was only 10.
We made slogans uttering his name.
It was the sign of confidence.
If you do not have confidence, you have nothing in spite of having everything.

Stupidity was taking place regarding Urdu.
Urdu was not a native language in any province of Pakistan.
The North-West Frontier Province's language was Pashto.
Baloch was a language for the Baloch province.

Millions of Muslims in the world speak in hundreds of languages.
What could be a language for a religion?
Is Urdu an Islamic one indeed?
Listening to it, I am irritated.

Bengali was the language for 66 percent of the people in Pakistan.
If the leader made a mistake and took the country in the wrong direction, the people had their right to protest it.
This is the rule of democracy.

Mr. Jinnah could be a leader.
Could he impose injustice on us?
No. He did not have the right.
How could he decide to make Urdu the state language?
We could not think of it.
We could not accept it.

The country was witnessing one wrongdoing after another.
The country was also experiencing growing riots and food shortages.
Excessively vigilant government officers were torturing the poor and collecting money.

How could I witness it?
How could I bear it?
The poor cried in pain…
The poor died…
Pakistan was blamed.

Mr. Suhrawardy and I tried to protect community harmony.
The government did not take it positively, and they took an opposing view.
They assigned detective officers against us.

"Where was our destination?"
They misinterpreted our political stance.
The leader who founded Pakistan had no way to survive in Pakistan.
What would be the fate of this country?
This was the situation of Mr. Suhrawardy.

I am not a man to flee.
I will continue protesting injustice.
I will see the end of this country and life.

Mr. Jinnah died on September 11, 1948.

Nazimuddin became the governor and Nurul Amin became
the Chief Minister.
Who could bar them anymore?
They excluded Mr. Suhrawardy from the Public Assembly.
This is Nazimuddin.
This is Nurul Amin.
What does power mean?
What does meanness mean?
A conspiracy continued against the Bengali language.
If Bengali was not recognized as the state language, our culture
and civilization would vanish.
The songs that we loved would lose their dignity and relevance.
Bengali had been recognized as a state language.

Pakistan was made.
The fourth-class employees at Dhaka University began to
experience oppression.

They did not have job security.
They did not have accommodation.
The number of students grew.
The volume of work grew.
But the number of employees did not increase.
This situation continued.
In this situation I, along with some students, became involved
in the movement of the fourth-class employees.

We called a strike.
I was arrested for my involvement in this movement.
The movement intensified.

In 1947, the people from Bengal enthusiastically supported the Muslim League.

Within two years, the people rejected this party.

Why?

Because of bad rule, oppression, abuse and lack of an economic plan.

June 23, 1949.

I was in jail.

The East Pakistan Awami Muslim League was formed.

Moulana Bhasani was made president, Shamsul Haq became its secretary and I was chosen as its joint secretary.

There was no need for a communal name for a political party after the creation of Pakistan.

We understood.

But the time had not yet been ripe to use a non-communal name.

Considering this consequence, the word 'Muslim' was added with 'Awami League'.

This was my thought while I was in jail.

I was freed from jail.

Mr. Shamsul Haq gave me an idea that this was the time to launch our movement.

The country had become independent, but suffering had not disappeared.

Political activists were facing harassment without any judicial trial.

The government built industrial factories in West Pakistan.

On the other hand, East Pakistan witnessed the food crisis.

What were the people of Bengal doing?
How could we survive?

I had a conversation with my father and my wife Renu.
I opened my mind to them.
Without a powerful opposition party, democracy could not
exist.
But the Pakistan Muslim League did not accept this truth.

The Muslim League government declared Section 144 and
disrupted our public meetings.
When Mr. Moulana Bhasani raised his hands, we all raised
our hands.
Police officers and sepoys raised their hands.
Moulana Bhasani uttered all his political speeches through
his prayers.

Terrorists from the Muslim League inflicted many injustices.
We faced all this with our courage.

They had to face 'tit for tat.'
What would be the punishment for killing hundreds of people
as opposed to where one is hanged for murdering one person?
They deserved the death penalty by firing squad.
Liaquat Ali Khan, let him come and see what the people from
Bengal wanted.
We held a rally and made slogans for the freedom of the
people in Bengal.
Police attacked the rally.
Many of us were arrested and I was injured.

Moulana Bhasani had instructed me to avoid arrest.

But, I am not fond of secret politics.
I do not believe in secret politics.

Liaquat Ali Khan did not become the Prime Minister for the people.
Rather he turned to be a Prime Minister for one party.
He respected democracy, but he did not tolerate the opposition's opinion.
It could not be accepted.

What is the reason?
Why will I hide?

Moulana Bhasani told me: "You may go to Lahore.
Mr. Suhrawardy is in Lahore now."
I could reach Lahore using strategies and after facing huge troubles.

I was weakened by the bitterness of winter.
Mr. Suhrawardy asked whether I was in need of anything.
I responded saying, "No I do not need anything."
I knew his financial situation.

He bought a blanket, socks, sweater and muffler after a long search.
He dropped them at my hotel from the market.
He gifted me the winter clothes and said, "These are for you."
This was the quality of Mr. Suhrawardy.

I could not speak Urdu.
By mixing Bengali and Urdu, I spoke a hotchpotch language.

Then, I left Lahore for home.
I said good bye to Mr. Suhrawardy.
I felt empty.

When would we meet again?
Who knows?
Who can tell?

I came to Calcutta from Lahore via Delhi.
I needed to be careful on the train.
I put on disguises, moving in the guise of a porter.
I wore a lungi in a shorter form, just as a porter does.
I carried my luggage on my back and a bag in my hand.
The detective officers did not know my address.
They could not detect my trace.

Mr. Huq and others in jail lived with torture.
I did not have peace in my mind.
I would not get peace in their company.
Would I go to jail?

Arriving in Gopalganj, I took a ride on a rickshaw.
The driver hailed from Gopalganj.
I could trust him.
He wanted to know about me and I could tell him.

The illusion for Renu and our children grew.
At that point, I had dedicated myself to the service of our
country.

I had made a commitment for sacrifice.
I had to go to Dhaka leaving Tungipara.

Renu wanted to go to Dhaka.
She wanted to live with me.
I did not give my consent.
Where could she live in Dhaka?
I did not want to give any trouble to my relatives.

I started from our home at night.
If I started by day, Hasina woud cry.
Kamal was also old enough to understand the consequences.
At the time of my departure, I also saw tears in Renu's eyes.
What new could I tell her?
I had told her everything.

I reached Dhaka taking many different paths.
Next day, just as I was ready to eat my lunch the Police reached there too.
What can I tell you?
"I was waiting for your arrival."

At this point in the story I remember, Mr. Moulana Bhasani,
Mr. Shamsul Haq were in jail.
The condition of Mr. Shamsul Haq began to deteriorate.
He shouted at any time of day or night for hours.
His hues and cries were in the name of Allah.
We did not have any alternative but to accept his shouts.
We tolerated it.

Liaquat Ali Khan was the Prime Minister of Pakistan.
Nurul Amin was the Prime Minister of East Bengal.
The level of oppression had crossed its limit.

1949.
Prisoners sat on hunger strike for 200 days out of 365 days
that year.
The Muslim League, for the sake of power, tortured the people.
Liaquat Ali Khan wanted to run the country inciting conflict
between the Bengalis and the Punjabis.
Exactly what the British did.

Nurul Amin was Bengal's Prime Minister only by name.
Power lay in the hands of bureaucrats.
Nurul Amin just followed their instructions.

We were in jail.
Who would speak for us?
Mr. Suhrawardy gave a statement for us.
The newspapers published this statement.

The health of Mr. Shamsul Haq deteriorated.
Mr. Moulana's Ittefaq was shut down.
He asked journalist Manik Miah, whom I address as Manik
Bhai, to run the Ittefaq.

Towards the end of 1950, Mr. Moulana and Mr. Shamsul Haq
were released from jail.
Mr. Moulana returned to jail again.

I was placed in a single dark room in jail.
Why?
For giving me suffering and pain.
What a suffering it was.
Can anyone unless being a sufferer understand it?

They released me.
At the same time, they arrested me.
What barbaric thoughts can live in them!

There are many Hindus in this country who honour people as
human beings.
They rushed to the people in danger.

1951.
The country witnessed community riots again.
I began a hunger strike in jail by demanding my release.
Injustice was everywhere — in the workplace, in business and
so on.
Now they started to impose injustice on the Bengali language.

I went on hunger strike.
The jail authority pushed food by a pipe through my nose.
They would not even let me die.

My nose was damaged
I lost weight, and my heart was irregular.
I had no energy to get up from bed.
It was painful even to breathe

February 21, 1952.
Dhaka experienced a heavy chaos.

"We demand for the release of political prisoners."
"We demand for the release of Sheikh Mujib."

I was worried.
"How many people have died in Dhaka?"
It was difficult for me to know then.

It was a situation, when great numbers of students started to
gather and chant slogans.
Under-aged boys and girls came out in the streets to chant
slogans.

It was an outcome of lacking in foresight.
Even a leader like Jinnah could not return without
witnessing the protest of the people at his speech in favour
of Urdu as the state language.

What would be the fate of Mr. Khawja and his allies in this
situation?
A group was engaged in conspiracy.
The people in this conspiracy were creating a situation to
make a distance between Jinnah and the people.
Simultaneously his supporter Nurul Amin had been detached
from the people.
Police had been out of order.

"I can imagine the face of Renu.
What will happen to Renu?
She has nobody on this earth.
What will happen to our two small children?"
I could not even see my children once.
I could be alive at least for one or two days more.

The doctor came and said to me, "Would you go if you were
released?'"
"If I am released, I will go,
Otherwise, I will not go —
But my dead body will be released."

The jailer read out the order of my release.
I did not want to believe it.
Previously they made such a farce with it.

A dedicated worker for our country, a dedicated leader
became mad as an outcome of his long jail life in a dark
room in custody.
To whom could I tell of this tale of sorrows?
The man who worked for the movement to create Pakistan,
he was made mad in Pakistan's jail.
Despite many attempts, I could not ensure treatment for
Mr. Shamsul Haq.

I contested an election.
The poor prayed for me.
They helped me to their best level.
I took up a pledge in my mind that I will never in my life
cheat the poor.

What is the use of religion in politics?
Fraudulent and deceptive Mollahs made their fatwas one after
another.
They declared in a fatwa that if people would vote for me,
Islam would be destroyed.
What a treacherous campaign.

No political party on this earth has experienced such a defeat.

It is a long practice for their class interest that the capitalists
use the poor workers, engaging them in riot and conflicts.
In return, the capitalists gain benefit.

Who protests against the unjust decision made by the central
government?
Some dare, some flee in fear.

I was taken to jail again.
I told my leaders and activists:
"Do not accept this unjust order silently and without protest.
You will oppose it publicly.
This country's people are ready.
You just have to lead them.
Many of us must go to jail,
it is better to go to jail after having protested."

What could I tell Renu?
The Police arrested me.
Our activists cried
I said, "Why are you crying?
This is my path indeed.
One day I will get out."

The Magistrate asked me where my colleagues were.
I told him I would not tell them even if I knew.

What hope did they nurture in their minds?
That I would tell secrets about my colleagues to them!

I was in jail.
We did not have anybody who could give a statement for me.
Mr. Bhasani was in London.
Mr. Suhrawardy was at a hospital in Zurich.

The people attacked the jail.
They picketed jailers' homes.
After learning the news, I rushed to the spot and calmed them
down.
I expected to get thanks.
Instead the authority filed a case against me.

Where do we go if this is the character of Pakistan?
Will I flee?
Sheikh Mujib is not a man to flee.

Why did the jailers shoot coming out of their complex?
Why were innocent people killed in those shootings?

Case after case continued.
They could not find any witness against me.

The one who is a thief behaves like a saint.
The one who thwarts attempts of theft faces trouble.
By dint of power, they put me in jail.
I do not care about such an administration.

Government's detective officers followed me.
They had an ambition to collect a bond from me.
I told them if it was a need, the government had given a
bond to me.
Without trial they should not keep me in jail.

What could I do?
It is natural that a leader without understanding, without a
discussion with his people, loses his importance?
Did I have any choice but to be upset and angry?
After his return from Germany, Mr. Suhrawardy became
Law Minister instead of being Prime Minister.
I did not contact him.
I did not even send him a telegram.
I did not need to.

The conspirators gained their benefit from conspiracy.
Jail was my fate.
I entered jail and was released from jail.
Where were my dear and near relatives?
Where were my life-mate, my children, siblings and parents?

This is life!
Jail had been a place of pilgrimage.
I got out of jail and went into jail.

West Pakistani rulers wanted even to change the name of
Bengal.
But why?
They wanted Bengalis to forget their name.
There would remain only soil in Bengal.
It was their motto.

They were so afraid of the name of Bengal.
"If I speak Punjabi Islam will not vanish.
If I speak Sindhi Islam will not vanish.
If I speak Urdu Islam will not vanish.
If I speak Bengali Islam will vanish."

They felt irritated when they heard Bengali sounds.
Belief might have had its logic or not.
But Language, Culture and Nationality are not easy matters.
I said, "Our country is Bengal, let yourselves call us Bengal."
They denied it.
They did not pay attention to me.

It should not continue.

Politics in Pakistan went under control of civil and military
bureaucracy.

After the Second World War, national leadership in many
countries had been established.
On the other hand, what a fate we had.

In 1952, without any reason, the Police fired bullets.
In the elections in 1954, we won.
But they conspired and did not let Mr. Suhrawardy and
Mr. Fazlul Huq function.
They did not let the United Front government survive.

Pakistan got her constitution.
Along with Urdu, Bengali was recognized as state language.

What a fate, Bengali has had!
In our long expected Pakistan, even communism is banned.
Even our Kabiguru Rabindranath Tagore is banned.

It is a fact that they want to oppress the Bengalis.
Through repeated oppression, General Ayub Khan declared
Martial Law.

Military Generals took over the power of Pakistan.
What else remained?
The gatekeeper took charge of house at gun point.

Progressive socialist politics were introduced in different
countries.
Because of our progressive leadership, we could hope too.

Mr. Suhrawardy passed away.
Mr. Bhasani left the Awami League.
I was all alone.

Except for Mr. Suhrawardy, no leader could feel the pulse of
Bengalis.

I have learned from Mr. Suhrawardy.
I will go forward following the path he showed me.
I will see who stops me.
I will choose the path of truth.
I will take a life risk.
Whether I win or lose, I have no need to hesitate.

Sheikh Mujib, painting by Nisar Hossain.

I was hopeful, I was dreaming.
My indomitable youth made me hopeful for an independent
Bengal, a free Bengal.
I buzzed and sang, 'We shall overcome one day.'

The ruling elites could not gain because of my firmness.
We were getting public support.
Jail was my second home.

People became furious, they began a movement —
"Kick and break the locks
of all the jails."
And so they went on…

Bengali's Six Points, Agartala Conspiracy Case, Students'
Eleven Points —
these were nothing but the gradual steps for people's freedom.

West Pakistani rulers chose assaults, cases and conspiracy
against us.
Military Generals were crocodiles of power.
They smelled conspiracy in everything.
Their noses did not know how to find a good smell.
They could not hear good words.
Good thinking did not exist in their brains.

I was mostly in jail.
My daughter grew up.
She got married too.
My daughter along with her husband came to see me in jail.
What could I give them as gifts?
How could I bless them?
I gifted my wrist-watch to my son in law Wajed.
I paid obeisance by hugging my daughter Hasina.

The case against me continued.
Who would speak for me?
Who else was available except Bhasani?
None except him.
No journalist came here.
Fear and fear.

Trial against me continued.
Hearing of the cases continued.
Journalist Faiz made his presence before the court in a way
as if he had not known me.
I said, "If you want to live in Bengal, you must know Sheikh
Mujib."

It turned rather better for me and Faiz.
The Generals got an idea that Faiz had not known me.
As a consequence, Faiz published one report after another in
the newspaper.

Who could be in this danger?
Who could recover me from this danger?
Who had the courage and the will?
If only Bhasani did something.

Bhasani called a public meeting on Paltan Ground.
In his speech in this public meeting he said, "Mr. Generals of
West Pakistan, release all the political prisoners, including
Sheikh Mujib.
Otherwise you are welcome to accept our Walaikum Assalam —
our good bye."

1969.
Bengal saw Mass Upsurge.
I was released.
Then one General quit.
And another General emerged.

The elections were held.
My political party Awami League, and I, won.

They did not pay attention to our words.
They did not hand over power to us.
Power is a disease to them.
They are handicapped by power.
They do not care what is right and what is wrong.
They do not know how to choose the right path.
They made excuses one after another.
They directed their conscience towards the evil ways.

Then?

The country was pushed into darkness.
Pakistani military fired on the people in cities.
The entire world was aware of this.
But they were shameless.
They lacked conscience.

I was arrested.
I was released.
I went to jail again.
It is difficult to understand whether I was going to jail or
getting out of jail.
That is why I always kept my bag packed.
Renu knew it.
Hasina knew it.
The people of my country knew it.

1971.

The 7th March approached.
What could I say, we discussed.
We had a meeting.
We discussed it.
Would I declare independence or not?
What would happen if I declared?
How would I formulate the declaration of independence if I
were to pronounce it?
How could I calm the public if I did not declare
independence?
What could I do?

Renu said,
"It is important for you to trust your knowledge.
You know everything, more than what others think and say.
You know your country's people well and understand them.
Taking all these considerations into account, it is better you
speak your mind spontaneously to the public in the meeting."

The Race Course Ground —

This time our struggle is for freedom.
This time our struggle is for our independence.

March 26, 1971.
In the early hours, I declared the Independence of Bangladesh
on East Pakistan Rifles' wireless.
The occupying Pakistani forces arrested me.

My allies all knew when and what they must do.
I had given all suggestions to Tajuddin.
I had given him instructions about when and with whom he
must communicate.

It would be good enough if Tajuddin could meet with Indira
Gandhi.
It would be a big danger if Tajuddin was arrested.

It was my strategy to be arrested.
If I were to flee, the Pakistani military could have spread a lot
of false propaganda.
And in search of me, they could have set the entire country
on fire.
Nobody else but Renu knew all these facts.

Many plans would have become easier if Tajuddin could meet
with Indira ji.
Support and cooperation from other countries and diplomacy
were greatly needed.
Indira ji could handle it.

We were afraid of America and China.
We could depend on Russia and Indira ji.
I had trusted on the Bengalis that they could tackle the
pressure from the United States of America and China.
Even if I were killed, the Bengalis could free my country from
enemies.
I have given them instructions on the March 7 and March 26.
So I had peace in my mind even if I should die.

I thought of Renu a lot.
What was Hasina doing?
Rehana, Kamal, Jamal, Russel — were they still alive?

Were they safe?
Could Hasina deliver her baby safely?
Was the new born a girl or a boy?
Where was Wajed?

I am in jail today.
I do not get any news.
I do not know any news about my country.

I remember many faces today.
I remember Mr. Suhrawardy.
I remember my father.
I remember the face of my mother.

Shamsul Haq somehow was released from jail as a mad person.
How is Mr. Bhasani?
Where is he now?
Who knows?

Could Tajuddin form the government?
Would the Pakistani soldiers win in the war?
No!
That could not be.

I would have been happy if the country was to become
independent.
It would have been matter of peace for me if the country was
freed from its enemies.

Kabiguru Rabindranath Tagore, Gandhi ji, Titumir, Haji
Shariatullah, saw us from heaven.
Pakistani soldiers jumped on the Bengalis, fired on them and
killed them.
Did the people in the world know this news?
Could they know it?

"When the Bengalis are ready to die
Nobody can stop them."

Whose message did I hear at dawn?
"There is no fear, no fear in fact.
Whoever will sacrifice his life at the end
He has no loss, no end.

The Bengalis will win.
For the sake of God."

I was in jail.
Many offerings.
Many questions.
Many fears.
Many threats.

Finally, the enemies could not succeed.
They could not.
I did not lose my trust in the Bengalis.

The Pakistanis even dug a grave for me inside the jail.
They played many tricks.

I did not get any news about my country.
I did not hear anything.

The General came.
Zulfikar Ali Bhutto came.
Then I could guess that they could not reach their goal.
They could not.

They wanted to come to an understanding with me.
They wanted to make a change in their strategies.
They wanted to stay together with us.

I said, "No commitment today.
Firstly, I want to go to my country.
I will talk to the people in my country.
Then I will tell you whether we would be together with you
or not."

From Pakistan to London.
London to Delhi.
Delhi to Dhaka.
Then in the independent Bangladesh.

I saw thousands of crowds in the streets from the airport to
the Race Course Ground.

We tried to rebuild our independent Bangladesh.
But they did not stop with the conspiracies.
Their greed had no end.
Big powers like America, Pakistan and China could not accept
our progress.
They did not want to see that we were well.
Conspiracies everywhere.
Enmity everywhere.
Forecast of danger.

I knew.
Renu understood.
My near ones understood.
Yet, I was approached in way as if I did not understand.

Mushtaq came as a friend.
He showed excessive love.
Excessive respect is a sign of having something bad in the mind.

Many could not accept our sovereignty.
They did not want us to remain well.
America had made a commitment to supply food.
They broke the commitment.
They returned their ship carrying food.

They got Basanti dressed in a fishing net.
They took her photo.
They showed the photo to the world.

Where can we go?
The Razakar forces, Mir Jafar, Golam Azam —
it is difficult to trust them.
What can we do without putting our trust in them?

We want to be in peace.
We want to have friendship.
We do not want enmity with anyone.

Allende's Chile and Sheikh Mujib's Bangladesh.
It is a surprising similarity.

I deliver my speech in Bengali in the United Nations.
The World can know Bangladesh is a language-based nation.

You know everything and
You understand everything. . .

Where is the end?

1975.

We want to have friendship.
They play tricks.
My country needs food.
They have food.
They play tricks even with people's life.
Forgetting their evil, we want to achieve peace.
We have decided to look forward together.

America sent food grains.
But the ship carrying food did not anchor at the seaport.
Rather they turned back.
Who benefited from this?
They?
They just wanted it.

People died in hunger.
The people in the world got to know that people die in hunger
in Sheikh Mujib's independent country.
I want to get away from problems.
We must introduce a system where no-one will have a chance
to make bad plans against us.

The poor will not die in hunger.
Our country is for all with different religions, different
opinions, various castes and beliefs.
This is a system for labourers, farmers and all professionals,
a socialist system that is called BAKSAL.

The country achieved independence in 1971.
But the conspiracy against us never stopped.
A group of people are always against us.
They want to stigmatize our reputation.
They want to leave a bad spot on our image.
Then they will stop.
I have no peace in my mind.

Tomorrow I will go to the Convocation at Dhaka University.
As the University Chancellor, I will address the students and
teachers.

In life, I have delivered many speeches at marketplaces, ports,
ships, boats, vans, trucks, buses and grounds and amidst the
sea of crowds.
But tomorrow, I will deliver my speech as a chancellor for the
first time.

I have many memories from this university, many processions.
Movements, strikes, arrests and warrants for arrests.
What many things.

The reality is different now.
We have expelled the British.
We have expelled the Pakistanis.
Now we have an independent Bangladesh.
I am leader of an independent country's poor people.
I am their President.

Tagore has said,
"Hello satisfied mother of seven crore Bengalis.
You have kept them as Bengali, you have not got them grown
up as human beings."
This is a time for us too to become human beings.
To go forward to a life in peace, in order and in relief.
Am I right, Renu?

"It is midnight, it is time to sleep," Renu says.
Yes, that's right.

Who is this?
Who is shooting here?

Where are you, Army Chief Shafiullah?
Your soldiers are shooting at my home.

Shafiullah suggests I flee from home somehow.

Hello,
is Sheikh Mujib a man to flee?
Have we achieved independence of our country only to flee
from it?

Why are you suggesting I go with you?
What do you want?

Why have you killed Kamal and Jamal?
Give me the answer?

Be cautious!
Don't shoot anyone else.

Hello,
stop it. I am asking you to stop it.

Why are you playing stupid with me?

Why are you even pointing guns at me.

What idiots you are!

Is that why I made this country independent?

EPILOGUE

Bangabandhu received bullets in his chest.
He fell down...

Sheikh Mujibur Rahma, *Asamapta Armajiboni* [Incomplete
      Autobiography], Dhaka 2012.
Faiz Ahmed, *Madhyarater Ashwarohi* [Horse Rider at
      Midnight], Dhaka 2015.
Sheikh Hasina, *Sheikh Mujib Amar Pita* [My Father Sheikh
      Mujib], Dhaka 2015.
Humayun Ahmed, *Deyal* [Wall], Dhaka 2014.
Swapan Dasgupta (Ed.), *Bangabandhu Hatya Mamla*
      Prathomik Tathyabiborani Theke Curanta Rae
      [Bangabandhu's Murder Case from the First
      Report to the Final Verdict], Dhaka 2010.
Nirmalendu Goon, *Raktajhora November 1975* [The Massacre
      in November 1975], Dhaka 2014.
Badruddin Umar, *Amaar Pita* [My Father], Dhaka 2014.
Sharmin Ahmad, *Tajuddin Ahmad: Neta o Pita* [Tajuddin
      Ahmad: Leader and Father], Dhaka 2015.
Moyeedul Hasan, *Muldhara 71* [Basic Principle –71], Dhaka
      2017.

I remember many faces today.
I remember Mr. Suhrawardy.
I remember my father.
I remember the face of my mother.
...
From Pakistan to London.
London to Delhi.
Delhi to Dhaka.
Then in the independent Bangladesh.

These lines are delivered towards the end of Anisur Rahman's monologue, written in the voice of Sheikh Mujibur Rahman. They are stanzas within this epic monologue that recall the exploration of central themes within this literary work. These themes include memory, imagination and reality, the essence of the now and an internationalism that maintains cultural respect while demanding equality; as well as an openness to differing religious views and the importance of language and its creative usage. This work intertwines two perspectives, of course, that of Rahman (the author and poet) and that of the father of the Bengali nation, Sheikh Mujib.

Rahman is prolific in several genres and this fusion of poetry and drama creates a unique voice. Intimate personal family recollection, detached historical statements and constant appeals to the social and political conscience of the reader/audience create an intensity that is almost unbearable.

The format/delivery then, becomes almost a stream of consciousness as well as conscience. Rahman plays with the concept of time. Almost the entire monologue is set in the present tense; whether that present is during the time of Sheikh Mujib's incarceration, during his childhood or in a present that is so contemporaneous to the reader's perspective that it becomes the future.

The monologue is littered with dates and significant political events presented dispassionately and irrefutably and so the proclamations of a great statesman and orator are allowed to hang on these, anchored firmly within the poetic narrative.

This is a time for us too to become human beings

The reader's responsibility in the future is evident, the importance of inclusivity of family in a universal sense and commitment to that in order to address worldwide inequality and poverty.

Give me the answer?

Even this demand carries a question mark. There are no answers here. We are given what we must accept as facts and constantly questioned what we will do to achieve the dream of this human being who was Sheikh Mujib.

Dominic Williams

ABOUT ANISUR RAHMAN

Bengali-Swedish writer Anisur Rahman's (b. 1978) authorship based in Bangladesh and Scandinavia. He is one of the board members of the Swedish Writers' Union.

His diverse literary works include prose, poetry, novels, short stories and books for children. His plays have been presented on the Swedish Radio Theatre, the Norwegian Radio Theatre, and at various universities and theatres in Africa, Asia and Europe.

Educated from Dhaka University and Stockholm University, Rahman works for the Uppsala Centre for Literature, where he also leads creative writing programmes. He is heavily involved in literary cultural debates in media houses like bdnews24.com, unt.se and anisur.net, etc.

Zaheer Ahmed, studies English at Dhaka University. He works as a copy editor for the Daily Business Standard, Dhaka.

Nisar Hossain (b. 1961) is a much admired and outspoken artist and Dean of the Faculty of Fine Arts at Dhaka University. He is a specialist on contemporary painting, art material, and folk painting. Hossain's work done on environmental, gender or anti-imperial issues have appeared on a global scale. He has had exhibitions in Zimbabwe, India, Germany, Sri Lanka, Denmark, USA, Japan, and Bangladesh.

Rafiqun Nabi (b. 1943), better known as Ranabi, is a Bengali artist and cartoonist. He was awarded Ekushey Padak in 1993 by the government of Bangladesh. He completed his bachelor's and master's from the East Pakistan College of Arts and Crafts (now Faculty of Fine Arts, University of Dhaka); and served as a faculty member of that faculty 1964-2010.

Melanie Perry is a poet and spoken word performer from Wales. Her poetry has appeared in a wide range of publications. She has two poetry collections, *Rum Dark Nights* (Three-Throated Press, 2017) and the bilingual *Sound the Hollow/ Det håligas ljud* (Magnus Grehn Förlag, 2018). She is co-director of write4word, based in Wales.

Dominic Williams, born in the valleys of the South Wales Coalfield, is a writer and poet based in Carmarthenshire, UK, where he runs his publishing house Iconau Books in the small fishing village of Ferryside on the Tywi estuary. Williams is co-founder of the community interest company write4word. With Irish poet Denis Collins, he established the Wales Ireland Spoken Word and Poetry Alliance (WISPA).

www.ingramcontent.com/pod-product-compliance
Lightning Source LLC
Chambersburg PA
CBHW030513130626
46549CB00007B/2976